From Poop to Profits

Launch Your Own Dog Waste Removal Business

Andrew Coleman

Introduction

The Growing Demand for Pet Waste Removal

Pet ownership is on the rise, with over 70% of U.S. households owning at least one pet. As more people integrate pets into their families, the need for specialized services like pet waste removal has increased significantly. For dog owners, the challenge of keeping a clean, sanitary outdoor space is a constant battle. Whether in private yards, shared apartment grounds, parks, or commercial spaces, managing dog waste efficiently is critical to maintaining clean environments, protecting water supplies, and promoting healthier communities.

The problem isn't just about aesthetics. Dog waste is a known carrier of bacteria, parasites, and pathogens that can contaminate local water sources if not properly disposed of. Moreover, local governments and homeowners' associations (HOAs) are becoming stricter about pet waste management, imposing fines and regulations to encourage responsible cleanup. As awareness grows about these issues, more pet owners and property managers are turning to professional pet waste removal services, driving steady demand for this unique business model.

This increased need for pet waste management is where entrepreneurs like you have a fantastic opportunity. Whether you're serving individual homeowners, apartment complexes, or commercial properties, offering this essential service can position you at the heart of a growing market.

Why This Business Model Works: Recurring Revenue and Flexibility

The beauty of a pet waste removal business lies in its simplicity. The core service—scooping and properly disposing of dog waste—requires minimal equipment, has low operating costs, and generates consistent, recurring revenue. This makes the business highly scalable, allowing you to grow by adding more customers and expanding to new service areas without requiring significant additional investment.

The subscription-based model is a cornerstone of the industry's success. Most customers opt for weekly or bi-weekly service, creating reliable cash flow and making it easier to predict revenue. Since pet waste management is a year-round necessity, you avoid the seasonality that affects many other service-based businesses. Even in winter, clients need their properties cleaned to prevent buildup, meaning you can maintain a steady income throughout the year.

Another appealing aspect of this business is the freedom it offers. You can run it solo or hire employees as you grow, giving you the flexibility to work part-time or full-time, depending on your needs. Since you control your schedule, you can choose the days and hours that work best for you. This flexibility is a major draw for people looking to escape the rigidity of traditional 9-to-5 jobs while still building a profitable business.

Busting the Myths: It's More Than Just Scooping Poop

At first glance, it's easy to underestimate the pet waste removal business. Many assume it's a low-skill, low-reward endeavor that's all about picking up poop. However, those who succeed in this field quickly discover it involves much more than that.

Running a pet waste removal service requires a combination of business savvy, customer service, and efficient operations management. From building a reliable client base to scheduling routes that minimize travel time, every aspect of the business demands strategic planning. Handling clients effectively—whether through friendly interactions or prompt issue resolution—is key to maintaining long-term contracts. Additionally, effective marketing plays a crucial role in distinguishing your business from the competition and creating a recognizable brand.

Moreover, proper waste disposal isn't as simple as bagging and tossing it into the nearest trash can. Depending on local regulations, you may need to transport waste to designated facilities or dumps. Some operators even explore eco-friendly disposal solutions, like composting (where regulations permit), adding a green edge to their business model.

The pet waste management business also offers opportunities for diversification. Many successful operators expand their services by offering deodorizing sprays, pet sitting, dog walking, or partnerships with animal shelters and HOAs. These additional services not only increase revenue but also strengthen customer relationships, making clients more likely to stay with your business over the long term.

The Opportunity Is Now

The pet waste removal industry is growing, and the timing couldn't be better to enter the market. With low startup costs, minimal barriers to entry, and increasing demand, starting a pet waste removal business offers a fast-track path to entrepreneurship. Whether you want to replace your full-time income or supplement your current earnings, this business provides a scalable, flexible way to build a thriving enterprise.

As you explore this guide, you'll discover everything you need to start, grow, and manage your own pet waste removal service. From pricing strategies and marketing tips to legal requirements and real-life success stories, this book covers every aspect of the business. The goal is to equip you with the tools, knowledge, and confidence to hit the ground running—whether you're scooping in your neighborhood or expanding to nearby cities.

If you've been searching for a business opportunity that's in demand, easy to start, and has real growth potential, look no further. The pet waste removal industry is waiting, and now is the time to grab a scoop and make your mark.

Business Structure and Legal Setup

Setting up the right business structure and meeting the necessary legal requirements are essential steps in launching your pet waste removal business. These decisions will affect your tax obligations, personal liability, and future scalability. In this chapter, we'll explore the different business structures, walk through the registration process, and discuss insurance options to keep your business protected.

Choosing the Right Structure: Sole Proprietorship vs. LLC vs. S-Corp

When starting your pet waste removal business, selecting the appropriate legal structure is one of the most important early decisions. Each structure has its pros and cons, particularly in terms of liability protection, taxation, and ease of setup.

1. Sole Proprietorship

A **sole proprietorship** is the simplest and most common business structure for small startups.

Pros:

- Easy and inexpensive to set up.
- No separate business taxes—profits and losses are reported on your personal tax return.
- Full control of the business with minimal paperwork.

Cons:

- Unlimited personal liability—your personal assets are at risk if

the business is sued or incurs debt.
- Harder to raise capital or scale the business.
- Limited ability to separate personal and business finances.

A sole proprietorship may be ideal for a solo pet waste removal operator, but the risk of personal liability makes it less appealing for those who plan to hire employees or expand.

2. Limited Liability Company (LLC)

An **LLC** offers a balance between simplicity and liability protection, making it a popular choice for small businesses.

Pros:

- Limited liability—your personal assets are protected from business debts and lawsuits.
- Pass-through taxation—profits are taxed on your personal income, avoiding corporate taxes.
- Flexibility to grow with minimal paperwork compared to corporations.

Cons:

- More paperwork and cost compared to a sole proprietorship.
- Requires annual fees and filings, depending on the state.
- Complexity increases if you have multiple owners.

The LLC structure is an excellent fit for those who want to protect their personal assets without dealing with the complexities of forming a corporation.

3. S-Corporation (S-Corp)

An **S-Corp** is a tax designation available to LLCs and corporations, offering certain tax advantages for profitable businesses.

Pros:

- Avoids double taxation—profits are taxed only at the shareholder level, not at the corporate level.
- Shareholders can receive distributions that may not be subject to self-employment taxes.
- Limited liability, like an LLC.

Cons:

- Requires more paperwork and formalities (e.g., bylaws, shareholder meetings).
- Limited to 100 shareholders, and shareholders must be U.S. citizens or residents.
- State-specific fees and compliance requirements.

An S-Corp may be worth considering if your business grows to the point where tax savings on self-employment income become significant.

Key Takeaway:

If you plan to start small, a sole proprietorship or LLC is likely sufficient. However, if you foresee expanding your operations or hiring employees, consider forming an LLC for added liability protection and flexibility. Consulting with an accountant or attorney can help you determine the best structure for your specific goals.

Registering Your Business and Obtaining a Business License

Once you've chosen a structure, the next step is to register your business and ensure you comply with state and local regulations. The requirements will vary by state, but here are the general steps.

1. **Choose a Business Name:**
   Make sure your business name is unique and doesn't conflict with existing businesses. Most states have online search tools to check name availability.
2. **File the Necessary Paperwork:**
   - **Sole Proprietorship:** Register your business name (if different from your own) with your county or state.
   - **LLC or Corporation:** File the Articles of Organization (LLC) or Articles of Incorporation (corporation) with your state's Secretary of State office.

1. **Apply for an EIN (Employer Identification Number):**
   Even if you don't plan to hire employees, an EIN from the IRS is often required to open a business bank account. You can apply for an EIN online through the IRS website for free.
2. **Obtain a Business License:**
   Many cities and counties require businesses to obtain a general business license. Check with your local government to determine if you need one and how to apply.
3. **Check for Additional Permits:**
   Depending on your location, you may need specific permits for waste disposal or transportation, especially if you plan to haul waste to a landfill or dump site.
4. **Open a Business Bank Account:**
   Keeping your business and personal finances separate is essential, especially if you've chosen an LLC or corporation structure.

Pro Tip:

When selecting a name, avoid humorous or novelty names if you plan to work with HOAs, property managers, or commercial properties—clients may prefer a more professional-sounding business.

Insurance Requirements: General Liability, Vehicle Insurance, and More

Running a pet waste removal business involves certain risks, and having the right insurance coverage will protect you from unforeseen events. Here are the key types of insurance to consider:

1. General Liability Insurance

General liability insurance covers your business against claims of bodily injury or property damage. For example, if you accidentally damage a customer's fence or a client trips on equipment you left in their yard, this insurance will help cover the costs.

- **Coverage:** Property damage, bodily injury, and medical expenses.
- **Cost:** Typically $500–$1,000 annually, depending on coverage limits.

2. Vehicle Insurance

If you use your personal vehicle for business purposes, your personal auto insurance may not cover accidents that occur while working. A **commercial vehicle insurance policy** ensures you're protected while driving between jobs.

- **Coverage:** Property damage, bodily injury, and theft or damage to business equipment stored in the vehicle.
- **Cost:** Varies based on vehicle type, coverage, and location.

3. Workers' Compensation Insurance

If you plan to hire employees, most states require you to carry **workers' compensation insurance**. This coverage provides benefits to employees who are injured on the job, helping cover medical expenses and lost wages.

- **Coverage:** Medical expenses, lost wages, and rehabilitation services for injured employees.
- **Cost:** Based on the number of employees and the nature of the work.

4. Professional Liability Insurance

This insurance, also known as **errors and omissions (E&O) insurance**, protects your business from claims of negligence or unsatisfactory work. Although not required for pet waste removal, it may be useful if you offer additional services like pet sitting or dog walking.

5. Umbrella Insurance

If you want additional protection beyond the limits of your general liability and vehicle insurance, consider an **umbrella insurance policy**. This coverage provides an extra layer of security, especially as your business grows and takes on more clients.

Conclusion

Choosing the right business structure and ensuring you meet legal and insurance requirements are critical steps to building a strong foundation for your pet waste removal business. While a sole proprietorship might work for a small operation, an LLC offers better protection and scalability for long-term growth.

Registering your business, obtaining the necessary licenses, and securing insurance coverage will safeguard your operations and give you peace of mind. With these legal and structural elements in place, you'll be ready to focus on growing your client base, managing operations, and delivering excellent service.

Taking the time to set up your business correctly from the start will save you headaches down the road, allowing you to concentrate on what really matters—building a successful and thriving pet waste removal business.

Creating a Business Plan

You Might Not Need It for Funding, But You Still Need It for Success

Even though you're likely funding this business yourself and not seeking loans or investors, a business plan is still an essential tool. Think of it as a **roadmap**—a way to stay on course and keep your goals in focus. Without a plan, you may find yourself lost in the day-to-day tasks, unsure how to grow, manage operations efficiently, or handle unexpected challenges. A solid business plan helps you lay out exactly how you'll run your pet waste removal business and identify steps to scale or pivot as needed.

A business plan isn't just for financial institutions—it's a **blueprint** to guide your decision-making and keep you on track as your business develops. Whether you're launching as a solo entrepreneur or planning to build a team, a plan will help you visualize your goals, track your progress, and ensure you don't overlook key elements of your operations.

Setting Your Goals and Financial Projections

Establishing clear goals is the first step toward ensuring your business is sustainable. Your goals might focus on several areas: the number of clients, revenue growth, operational efficiency, or expansion into new markets.

Short-Term Goals (3–6 Months):

- Acquire your first 10–20 clients.

- Establish a streamlined route to maximize efficiency.
- Break even by covering equipment, fuel, and marketing expenses.
- Develop a system for customer communication and invoicing.

Long-Term Goals (1–3 Years):

- Expand to 50+ regular clients or multiple territories.
- Hire and train employees to manage operations.
- Add complementary services (e.g., yard deodorizing, pet sitting).
- Scale operations to other cities or offer commercial contracts with HOAs or apartment complexes.

Financial Projections

Even in a small-scale business like pet waste removal, financial projections are essential. They allow you to monitor your cash flow, set realistic revenue goals, and plan for growth. When creating your financial forecast, include:

- **Startup Costs:** Initial investment in equipment, insurance, marketing, and permits.
- **Monthly Expenses:** Gas, vehicle maintenance, trash bags, insurance, and any software subscriptions.
- **Revenue Forecast:** Estimate how many clients you'll serve and the fees they'll pay (e.g., $45/month per household).
- **Profit Margins:** Keep an eye on how much of your revenue is left after paying expenses. Many pet waste businesses boast high margins since operating costs are relatively low.

A business plan helps you assess whether your revenue will comfortably exceed your costs and allows you to experiment with pricing structures before committing to them in the real world. **Tracking your actual performance against your projections** will enable you to identify areas where you can improve efficiency or adjust your goals.

Defining Services: Subscription Models vs. One-Time Cleanups

One of the major decisions you'll need to make in your business plan is how to structure your services. The pet waste removal business lends itself well to both **recurring subscription services** and **one-time cleanups**, each offering distinct advantages.

Subscription Models

Subscription services provide **consistent, predictable income**—a critical factor in business stability. Customers pay a flat fee (usually monthly) for regular cleanups, which helps them avoid the hassle of managing waste themselves.

- **Example Pricing:**
    - $45/month for weekly service (1 dog)
    - $60/month for twice-a-week service
    - $15 per additional dog
- **Advantages:**
    - Predictable cash flow for easier financial planning.
    - Easier route planning with repeat clients.
    - Builds customer loyalty and trust through consistent service.
- **Potential Challenges:**
    - Requires efficient scheduling to keep costs down.
    - Some clients may cancel during slower seasons (e.g., winter).

One-Time Cleanups

One-time cleanups can be offered for **special occasions** or for customers who have fallen behind on yard maintenance. These are often priced higher due to the additional time and labor required.

- **Example Use Cases:**
    - Pre-party or post-party yard cleanup.
    - Large cleanups for new customers who have accumulated waste over time.
    - Special events or one-time service before home inspections.

- **Advantages:**
    - Higher profit margins on individual jobs.
    - Flexibility—fits into gaps in your regular schedule.
    - Great way to attract new clients who may convert to subscriptions.
- **Potential Challenges:**
    - Less predictable income stream.
    - Requires more marketing to attract new customers regularly.

Combining Subscription and One-Time Services

Many successful pet waste removal businesses **offer both models** to maximize revenue. For example, you could start with a one-time cleanup for new customers and offer a discount if they sign up for a monthly subscription. This not only increases your chances of securing regular clients but also **smooths out income fluctuations**.

Pro Tip: Offering add-on services—such as yard deodorizing or pet waste station installations—can boost revenue and differentiate your business from competitors. For example, you might offer a premium "odor elimination" service for an additional $10 per month or sell pet waste disposal stations to HOAs and apartment complexes.

Creating a Simple Business Plan Template

Your business plan doesn't need to be overly complicated. Below is a sample outline to get you started:

Business Plan for [Your Business Name]

1. **Executive Summary**
   A brief overview of your business goals, services offered, and target market.
2. **Business Structure and Legal Setup**
   - Structure: LLC, Sole Proprietorship, or S-Corp.
   - Licenses, permits, and insurance.
3. **Services Offered**
   - Subscription plans (weekly or bi-weekly).
   - One-time cleanups (special events, large accumulations).
   - Add-on services (yard deodorizing, waste station installation).
4. **Market Analysis**
   - Target audience: Pet owners, HOAs, property managers.
   - Competitor analysis: Pricing, services, and market gaps.
5. **Marketing Strategy**
   - Social media campaigns and local advertising.
   - Partnering with vets and animal shelters.
6. **Operational Plan**
   - Route planning and scheduling.

- ○ Equipment needed and maintenance schedule.

7. **Financial Projections**
   - ○ Startup costs and monthly expenses.
   - ○ Revenue forecasts based on number of clients and service frequency.
   - ○ Profit margins and break-even analysis.

Conclusion

While you may not need a formal business plan to secure funding, taking the time to create one will set you up for long-term success. A well-thought-out plan provides a **roadmap for your business** and ensures you stay focused on your goals. It will help you determine which services to offer, how to manage finances effectively, and how to scale the business as demand grows.

By identifying the services that make sense for your market—whether it's a mix of subscription models and one-time cleanups—you'll position yourself to meet customer needs while building a sustainable, profitable business. As your business evolves, your plan can evolve with it, providing clarity and direction along the way.

Equipment and Startup Costs

One of the biggest advantages of starting a pet waste removal business is that **the equipment needs are minimal** and initial costs are low. Unlike many other service-based businesses, you don't need specialized tools, expensive vehicles, or complex technology. In fact, your business can be up and running with just a few essential items. This chapter will walk you through what you need, what's optional, and what to consider as you grow your business.

Scooping Tools, Bags, and Transport Solutions

To start your pet waste removal business, **all you really need are a few simple tools**. Many pet waste businesses keep things straightforward, opting for basic scooping equipment, bags, and minimal extras. Below are some essential tools:

Essential Tools:

1. **Pooper Scoopers or Rakes:**
   - Opt for long-handled scoops or rakes so you don't need to bend down.
   - Metal scoops are more durable, while plastic ones are lightweight and affordable.
2. **Heavy-Duty Trash Bags:**
   - Large bags (13-gallon or larger) work well for collecting waste.
   - Many businesses use **regular trash bags from bulk retailers** like Costco or Sam's Club.
3. **Protective Gloves:**
   - Disposable gloves or reusable rubber gloves keep

things sanitary.
- ○ Not strictly necessary but recommended for larger cleanup jobs.
4. **Footwear:**
   - ○ Comfortable, waterproof shoes or boots will keep you protected and comfortable throughout the day.

Waste Disposal Options:

Some pet waste businesses **dispose of collected waste directly in the client's trash bins**. This reduces your need for storage or transport solutions, keeping things simple and cost-effective. If this is your approach, you **won't need waste buckets or separate transport containers** on your vehicle.

- **Alternative Disposal:**
  If you choose to transport waste off-site (e.g., for commercial clients), you may need **sealable buckets** or trash bins for the vehicle. This method adds a step to your process but can appeal to clients who don't want the waste in their bins.

Vehicle Considerations: Mileage, Fuel Costs, and Wear and Tear

While you don't need a specialized vehicle to run a pet waste removal business, your vehicle will still play a central role. **Whether you're driving a personal car, truck, or van**, it's essential to factor in the operational costs associated with mileage and fuel.

Key Considerations:

- **Fuel Costs:**
  - ○ Plan your routes carefully to minimize fuel usage. Many successful operators aim to **group clients by neighborhood** to

keep driving time under 5 minutes between stops.

- **Mileage and Wear and Tear:**
  - Regular vehicle maintenance is essential to prevent breakdowns. You'll want to account for oil changes, tire replacements, and other routine services in your budget.
  - **Tracking mileage** for business use can help you claim deductions at tax time, which is a useful way to offset some of your fuel and maintenance expenses.

- **Insurance:**
  - If you use your vehicle primarily for business, check with your insurance provider to see if you need to adjust your policy or purchase additional coverage.

Optional: Deodorizing Spray and Customer Gifts

While the basic pet waste removal business doesn't require much beyond scooping tools, bags, and a vehicle, **some optional extras can help set your business apart**. These small touches can improve the customer experience and give your business a more professional image.

Deodorizing Spray:

A **yard deodorizing spray** can be offered as an add-on service to help combat odor, especially in warmer months. Some businesses charge a small additional fee for this service, while others include it in premium service packages.

- **Examples:**
  - Spraying down areas affected by pet urine to neutralize odors.
  - Offering a free spray as part of a first-time cleanup to encourage clients to upgrade to a premium package.

Customer Gifts:

Simple, thoughtful gestures—such as leaving **treats for dogs** or **thank-you notes**—can go a long way toward building customer loyalty.

- **Dog Treats:**
  - Some scoopers keep small dog treats on hand to reward friendly pets.
  - This helps build a positive relationship with the pets you encounter and can increase client satisfaction.
- **Thank-You Cards:**
  - Periodically leaving a note or card with your service report can show clients you care.
  - These personal touches encourage word-of-mouth referrals and build stronger relationships.

Startup Cost Estimates

The beauty of the pet waste removal business is that **your initial investment can be as low as a few hundred dollars**. Below is a rough breakdown of typical startup costs:

Item	Estimated Cost
Pooper scoopers/rakes	$20–$50 each
Trash bags (bulk pack)	$30–$50
Gloves (disposable or reusable)	$10–$30
Business cards or flyers	$50–$100
Deodorizing spray (optional)	$20–$40 per bottle
Dog treats (optional)	$10–$20
Vehicle maintenance/insurance	Varies

Total Startup Cost:

- **Bare minimum:** $60–$150

- **With extras (treats, deodorizing spray, etc.): $150–$300**

Note: These costs are estimates and will vary based on the quality of the products you purchase. You can always start with the essentials and add optional extras as your business grows.

Conclusion

Starting a pet waste removal business doesn't require a significant upfront investment. **With just a few essential tools and basic vehicle maintenance**, you can hit the ground running and begin serving clients. The flexibility of disposing of waste in your clients' trash bins keeps things even simpler, eliminating the need for extensive transport solutions. Optional extras—like deodorizing sprays and treats—are easy ways to **differentiate your business** and build customer loyalty over time.

With **minimal startup costs and high-profit margins**, pet waste removal is a low-barrier business that's accessible to almost anyone. By keeping your equipment needs simple and focusing on efficiency, you'll be able to **scale quickly and keep your expenses low** while building a reliable income stream.

Finding and Securing Clients

Finding clients is the lifeblood of any pet waste removal business. Fortunately, both **residential and commercial clients** have growing demand for these services, providing multiple opportunities for growth. This chapter explores where to start, marketing strategies that work, and how excellent communication can set you apart from the competition.

Residential vs. Commercial Clients: Where to Start

Choosing the right market focus can shape the direction of your business. **Residential clients** offer the benefit of predictable, recurring revenue, while **commercial clients** bring larger contracts but may involve more complex requirements.

Residential Clients

Residential pet owners are the most common starting point for pet waste removal businesses. These clients typically seek regular yard clean-ups, often opting for **weekly or bi-weekly service plans**.

Advantages:

- **Recurring Revenue:** Weekly or monthly subscriptions ensure consistent cash flow.
- **Low Complexity:** Cleaning individual yards is usually straightforward.
- **Personal Relationships:** Positive client interactions encourage word-of-mouth referrals.
- **Minimal Equipment:** Residential services rarely require specialized tools.

Where to Find Them:

- **Neighborhood Facebook Groups**
- **Local Pet Owner Forums**
- **Flyers at veterinary clinics and dog parks**

Commercial Clients

Commercial clients may include **apartment complexes, homeowners' associations (HOAs), parks, pet-friendly businesses, and event organizers.** These clients often require larger-scale services but bring higher revenue opportunities.

Advantages:

- **Bigger Contracts:** Commercial agreements offer larger payouts.
- **Fewer Clients, Higher Impact:** A handful of large clients can sustain your business.
- **Brand Visibility:** Working with public spaces increases exposure.

Challenges:

- **More Complex Requirements:** Contracts may involve more negotiations and expectations.
- **Higher Standards:** Commercial clients may expect faster responses and additional services like deodorizing treatments.

Where to Find Them:

- **Property management companies and HOAs**
- **Partnerships with parks departments and pet-friendly hotels**

- **Networking with local businesses through chambers of commerce**

Marketing: Social Media, Flyers, and Partnering with Shelters

A strategic marketing plan is essential for attracting both residential and commercial clients. **Branding and visibility** are key—people need to see and trust your business before hiring you.

Social Media Marketing

Social media offers a powerful way to connect with potential clients and spread the word about your services.

- **Facebook & Instagram:**
    - Create a business page to post updates, promotions, and reviews.
    - Use Facebook groups to promote locally—many neighborhoods have dedicated groups for recommendations.
    - Run **targeted ads** on Facebook or Instagram to reach pet owners in your area.

- **Customer Reviews:**
    - Encourage happy customers to leave reviews. Positive testimonials on Google or Facebook are great for building trust.
- **Before and After Photos:**
    - Posting photos of cleaned yards (with permission) showcases the value of your service.

Flyers and Business Cards

Old-school marketing tactics like **flyers and business cards** can still be effective.

- **Flyers:**
    - Leave flyers at dog parks, veterinary clinics, pet stores, and grooming salons.
    - Focus on **clear, easy-to-read designs** that highlight your services and contact information.
- **Business Cards:**
    - Always carry business cards with you—they are great for networking and meeting potential clients on the go.

Partnering with Shelters and Animal Rescues

Animal shelters and rescue organizations often have **deep connections within the local pet community**. Partnering with these organizations can give your business credibility and provide direct access to potential clients.

- Offer to **donate a portion of your profits** to a shelter in exchange for being promoted to pet adopters.
- Volunteer for shelter events, where you can **hand out flyers or business cards** to attendees.
- Partner with rescues to provide **discounts for pet adopters**, encouraging them to try your service.

Communication Strategies: Why Responsiveness Sets You Apart

In the pet waste removal business, communication and responsiveness play a vital role in **client retention and satisfaction**. Many pet owners appreciate fast, clear communication, and this is often where small businesses shine over their larger competitors.

Respond Quickly to Inquiries

Responding to messages and inquiries within **24 hours** can set you apart from competitors. Clients appreciate prompt communication and are more likely to choose a business that answers their questions quickly.

Tips for Fast Communication:

- **Use Texting and Social Media:** Many customers prefer texting or messaging over phone calls.
- **Set Up Auto-Responses:** If you can't respond right away, set up auto-replies to let clients know you'll get back to them soon.
- **Dedicated Business Line:** Consider using a business phone number to keep work and personal calls separate.

Clarity and Professionalism

Clear communication is essential when setting client expectations. Be upfront about your services, prices, and any policies around cancellations or rescheduling.

- **Service Agreements:** Provide written confirmation of services, especially for new clients or commercial contracts.
- **Text Reminders:** Send friendly reminders before service appointments to reduce missed visits.
- **Service Reports:** After each visit, leave a short service report (either on paper or via text) to let clients know you've been there.

Handling Complaints and Issues

No business is immune to occasional issues or complaints. When problems arise, the way you handle them can determine whether you retain the client.

- **Apologize and Act Quickly:** If a client expresses dissatisfaction, acknowledge the issue and work toward a resolution promptly.
- **Offer Incentives:** Providing a discount on future services or a small gift can help turn a negative experience into a positive one.
- **Stay Professional:** Always maintain a polite, professional tone, even if the client is frustrated.

Conclusion

Finding and securing clients is the most crucial part of your business, and there are multiple ways to approach it. Whether you focus on **residential or commercial clients**, having a clear strategy for marketing and communication will set you up for success. **Social media, flyers, and partnerships** with local pet organizations are powerful tools for attracting customers, while fast, clear communication will help you build trust and retain clients.

The pet waste removal business is built on **relationships and reliability**. If you **respond promptly, deliver great service, and build strong connections** with clients and partners, you'll create a steady stream of business and a growing list of loyal customers.

Pricing Your Services

Pricing your pet waste removal services correctly is essential to ensure profitability while remaining competitive. This chapter will guide you through calculating your service costs, share real-world pricing insights from Reddit users, and explore how to offer discounts, add-ons, and subscription plans to attract more clients and boost your revenue.

Calculating Costs: Frequency, Number of Dogs, and Yard Size

Several factors impact how you price your services, including the **frequency of visits, the number of pets, and the size of the yard**. Understanding these variables helps ensure your prices cover operational costs and generate profit.

1. Frequency of Visits

- **Weekly service:** Common for most clients; ideal for pet owners who want to keep their yards clean year-round.
- **Twice-weekly service:** Suitable for homes with multiple pets or clients who prioritize an odor-free yard.
- **One-time cleanups:** Ideal for pet owners needing a major cleanup, such as after winter or before a social event.

Pro Tip: Offer discounts to clients who opt for more frequent services, as this ensures recurring revenue.

2. Number of Dogs

Each additional dog creates more waste, which increases the time and effort required. Pricing can be structured based on the **number of dogs**, with incremental increases for each extra pet.

Example Pricing Model:

- **1 dog:** $15 per week
- **2 dogs:** $20 per week
- **3 dogs:** $25 per week

3. Yard Size

Larger yards require more time to cover, increasing labor costs. Although many providers charge based on the **number of dogs**, some businesses add fees for exceptionally large yards (over 1/4 acre) or complex landscapes.

Example Yard Surcharge:

- **Small to Medium Yard:** No additional fee
- **Large Yard (1/4 acre or more):** +$5 to $10 per visit
- **Extra-Large or Difficult Terrain:** Custom quote

Regional Pricing Examples from the Field (Based on Reddit Insights)

Based on real-world insights from Reddit users in pet waste removal, here are **regional pricing examples** to help you benchmark your services:

- **Nebraska**
  - **$45/month** for once-a-week service for one dog
  - Prices increase based on additional dogs or more frequent visits
  - Business owners report **$50 per hour revenue** during routes
- **Charlotte, NC**
  - **$125/month** for twice-a-week service for two dogs, with an added fee for disposal outside the homeowner's trash bin

- **Midwest City (~275,000 population)**
  - ◦ **$85/month** for once-a-week service for one dog
- **One-Time Cleanups:**
  - ◦ **Starting at $50 to $100** depending on yard size and level of buildup

From these examples, it's clear that **local market conditions and the population's willingness to pay** play significant roles in pricing strategies. Suburban areas may command lower fees, while urban areas with higher costs of living may allow higher pricing.

Discounts, Add-Ons, and Subscription Plans

Offering **discounts, add-ons, and subscription plans** can make your service more appealing while building customer loyalty.

Discounts

- **First-Time Client Discount:** Offer 10-20% off for new customers to attract business.
- **Referral Discounts:** Reward existing clients with a discount or free service when they refer new customers.
- **Multi-Service Discount:** Offer reduced rates for clients who purchase multiple services, such as waste removal and odor treatment.

Add-Ons and Upgrades

- **Odor Control Spray:** +$10 per visit to spray down the yard with deodorizer.
- **Dog Treats:** Provide a treat for each dog after service for an extra **$5 per month**.
- **Special Event Cleanups:** Offer one-time yard cleanups for

parties or holidays, starting at **$50-$150** based on yard size and location.

Subscription Plans

Subscription models encourage long-term commitment from clients, providing you with predictable income.

Sample Subscription Plans:

1. **Basic Plan (Weekly Service, 1 Dog):**
   - $60/month ($15 per week)
2. **Standard Plan (Twice-Weekly Service, 1 Dog):**
   - $110/month

1. **Family Plan (Weekly Service, 2-3 Dogs):**
   - $80-$100/month

Clients appreciate the convenience of automatic billing, so consider setting up **recurring payments through payment platforms** to encourage subscriptions.

Conclusion

Pricing your pet waste removal services strategically ensures you **cover costs, attract clients, and generate consistent revenue**. By considering factors like the number of pets, frequency of visits, and yard size, you can develop a pricing model that works for both you and your clients. Use insights from other operators in your region to **benchmark your prices** and adjust as necessary.

Offering **discounts, add-ons, and subscription plans** can further enhance your appeal to customers while locking in steady, predictable income. The right pricing strategy helps you strike the perfect balance between **affordability and profitability**, setting your business up for long-term success.

Route Planning and Scheduling for Maximum Efficiency

Time spent traveling between clients can quickly eat into your profits. Creating efficient routes will minimize fuel costs, reduce wear and tear on your vehicle, and allow you to serve more clients within a day.

Key Route Optimization Tips:

1. **Cluster Clients Geographically:** Group clients who are close together and assign them to the same day of the week. This reduces unnecessary driving and maximizes efficiency.
   - Example: Serve all clients in one neighborhood on Mondays and those in the adjacent area on Tuesdays.
2. **Limit Backtracking:** Plan your routes to move in one continuous direction, such as clockwise or counterclockwise. Avoid looping back to areas you've already covered.
3. **Schedule Clients by Traffic Patterns:** Factor in rush hours or road construction to avoid delays. If certain areas are congested during specific times, plan your visit for a quieter period.
4. **Consider Frequency:** Assign higher-priority clients (e.g., those with multiple dogs or odor control add-ons) to your schedule early in the day to ensure timely service.
5. **Build in Buffer Time:** Allow for short breaks or unexpected delays between clients to stay on schedule.

Example:

If you have 10 clients in a day, with each property requiring 15-20 minutes, you can organize your route to keep travel time between stops to no more than 5-7 minutes. This ensures you finish within a typical 8-hour day.

Tools for Scheduling: Google Maps, CRM Systems, or PoopNET Alternatives

Having the right tools can make a significant difference in planning routes, managing schedules, and ensuring customer satisfaction.

Google Maps: The Simple, Free Option

- **Route Planning:** Google Maps allows you to input multiple stops and rearrange them for optimal routing.
- **Real-Time Traffic Updates:** Helps you avoid delays and adjust routes on the go.
- **Location Sharing:** You can save frequent addresses to a list, making it easier to plan recurring routes.

Pro Tip: Use **Google My Maps** to create custom maps with saved client locations for better route visualization.

CRM Systems for Small Businesses

Customer Relationship Management (CRM) software can help you stay organized with scheduling, billing, and customer communications. Here are a few user-friendly options for small businesses:

1. **Jobber:** Designed for field service businesses, Jobber provides route planning, invoicing, and customer management.
2. **Housecall Pro:** Offers scheduling, dispatching, and payment tracking, ideal for solo operators or teams.
3. **Zoho CRM:** A more customizable platform with client tracking and scheduling features.

These systems can sync with **Google Calendar** or **Outlook** to keep your schedule accessible on all devices.

PoopNET Alternatives

If you plan to grow your business, specialized tools like **PoopNET** (used by DoodyCalls) or other custom CRMs can streamline your operations. While PoopNET isn't available outside the DoodyCalls franchise, you can achieve similar functionality with affordable tools that integrate **routing, invoicing, and inventory tracking**.

Managing Seasonal Work and Winter Operations

Seasonal changes can affect your workload, especially in areas with **harsh winters**. Planning for these fluctuations will help keep your business running smoothly year-round.

Winter Operations: Handling Snow and Ice

- **Adjust Your Schedule:** Snow-covered yards can make it difficult to locate waste. Consider shifting some clients to bi-weekly service during heavy snow periods.
- **Charge for Post-Winter Cleanups:** After snow melts, yards often need a **deep cleaning** to remove accumulated waste. Offer this service at a higher rate.
  - Example: A post-winter cleanup might start at $75 or more, depending on yard size and buildup.

Communicate with Clients About Weather Delays:

Send automated texts or emails to inform clients of any delays or rescheduling due to severe weather. Offering clear communication builds trust and sets you apart from competitors.

Seasonal Promotions:

- **Pre-Winter Discounts:** Offer discounted rates to lock in new clients before winter hits, ensuring steady income during slower months.
- **Spring Cleanup Packages:** Promote one-time spring cleanups at the start of the season to attract new customers and boost cash flow.

Conclusion

Planning your routes and scheduling effectively is key to maximizing your productivity and profits. **Optimizing travel time, using scheduling tools, and preparing for seasonal challenges** will keep your operations running smoothly year-round. Efficient route planning also improves customer satisfaction, as clients will appreciate reliable, timely service.

By leveraging free tools like Google Maps or investing in **CRM systems** tailored to small businesses, you can streamline scheduling and focus more on growing your client base. With proactive planning, your business can thrive even during challenging winter months, setting you up for long-term success.

Managing Operations and Scaling the Business

Effective management and smart scaling strategies are essential for growing a sustainable pet waste removal business. This chapter will cover the core aspects of managing operations, handling customer service challenges, and scaling by expanding into complementary services like pet sitting and walking. Whether you choose to operate as a solo entrepreneur or grow into a multi-employee business, mastering these operational strategies will help ensure long-term success.

DIY vs. Hiring Employees or Subcontractors

As your business grows, you'll need to decide whether to continue doing the work yourself or hire employees or subcontractors. Each approach has its pros and cons, and the right choice will depend on your long-term goals, budget, and personal preferences.

Operating Solo (DIY)

- **Pros:**
    - Lower costs with no payroll or insurance requirements.
    - Full control over customer service and quality of work.
    - Easier to manage a small number of clients and keep things flexible.
- **Cons:**
    - Limited ability to grow, as there are only so many hours in a day.
    - No backup if you're sick or need time off.

- Risk of burnout from handling every aspect of the business alone.

Hiring Employees or Subcontractors

- **Pros:**
    - Enables faster growth and the ability to serve more clients.
    - Allows you to delegate labor-intensive tasks and focus on managing the business.
    - Provides continuity if you need time off or encounter emergencies.
- **Cons:**
    - Requires payroll, taxes, workers' compensation, and other employee-related expenses.
    - Training and managing employees take time and effort.
    - Quality control can become more challenging with multiple workers.

Tip: If you decide to hire employees, consider starting with **part-time help** or **subcontractors** to test the waters. This will allow you to scale without taking on too much risk at once.

Handling Customer Complaints and Refunds

Even with the best planning, occasional customer complaints are inevitable. How you handle them will shape your reputation and customer retention. Addressing complaints professionally and quickly can turn a frustrated client into a loyal one.

Strategies for Managing Complaints:

1. **Listen Actively:** Let the customer explain their concern fully

without interrupting. This shows that you care and helps you understand the issue.

2. **Apologize and Acknowledge:** Even if the complaint seems trivial, acknowledging the customer's frustration goes a long way.

Example:

"I'm really sorry for the inconvenience. Let me see how we can fix this."

1. **Offer Solutions:** Present solutions to resolve the issue, such as:
   - Re-cleaning the yard free of charge.
   - Offering a small discount on the next service.
   - Providing a refund if necessary (for legitimate issues).
2. **Follow Up:** After resolving the issue, follow up with the customer to ensure their satisfaction.

Tip: Use complaints as feedback to improve your operations. Track recurring issues and adjust your processes accordingly.

The Art of Upselling: Expanding into Pet Sitting, Walking, or Deodorizing Services

Once your core business is established, offering **complementary services** can increase revenue and improve customer satisfaction. Upselling additional services is an effective way to grow your income without needing to acquire new clients.

Complementary Service Ideas:

1. **Deodorizing Services:**
   - Spray yards with pet-safe solutions to eliminate odors.
   - Charge an **additional $10-$15 per visit** for deodorizing treatments, especially during warmer

months when odors intensify.

2. **Pet Sitting and Walking:**
   - Offer pet sitting or walking services to existing customers. Many pet owners prefer using trusted service providers they already know.
   - Charge **$20-$40 per walk** or **$50+ per day** for pet sitting, depending on your region.

3. **Holiday or Vacation Packages:**
   - Provide special packages for customers traveling during holidays. Offer yard cleaning and pet sitting combined at a discounted rate.
   - Example: A **$100 weekend package** that includes two scooping visits and a 30-minute walk each day.

4. **Referral Programs:**
   - Incentivize clients to refer their neighbors by offering **free services** or **discounts** for successful referrals.
   - Example: "Refer a friend and get your next scooping service free!"

Scaling Smartly: Setting the Foundation for Growth

As your client base grows, it's important to set up systems that allow you to scale without sacrificing quality or efficiency.

1. Use Technology to Your Advantage

Invest in tools like **CRM systems** (e.g., Jobber, Housecall Pro) to streamline scheduling, customer management, and invoicing. These systems reduce administrative work and free up time to focus on expansion.

2. Build a Brand Presence

- Develop a **professional website** and maintain active social media profiles to attract more customers.

- Use branded **vehicle wraps** to advertise your business as you drive from client to client.
- Establish yourself as a pet care authority by writing blogs, posting videos, or offering free advice on social media.

3. Expand Geographically or Offer New Services

- **Expand your service area**: Consider targeting nearby neighborhoods or towns.
- **Franchise your business**: If successful, explore the possibility of franchising your pet waste removal model.
- **Specialize in commercial accounts**: Offer services to apartment complexes, HOAs, and commercial properties that require regular maintenance.

4. Hire Smart

When you're ready to hire, focus on finding employees who share your commitment to quality and customer service. Provide **training** to ensure they meet your standards and know how to handle clients and animals.

Conclusion

Managing operations effectively and scaling your pet waste removal business requires a combination of **organization, customer service, and strategic growth efforts**. Whether you decide to keep it small and personal or grow into a multi-employee operation, the key to success is maintaining high service standards and staying responsive to customer needs.

Expanding into **complementary services** like pet sitting, walking, or deodorizing can unlock new revenue streams without requiring a significant investment. With the right systems, tools, and team in place, scaling your business becomes not only achievable but also a natural progression. By staying organized, listening to customer feedback, and leveraging upselling opportunities, you can build a thriving business that continues to grow and meet the needs of pet owners in your community.

Handling Pet Waste: Health, Safety, and Disposal

The ideal situation for handling pet waste is to dispose of it directly in the client's trash bin after scooping. This simple approach minimizes the need for transporting waste, reducing both effort and costs. However, some clients may prefer or request that the waste be removed from their property entirely. In those cases, it's important to understand the potential health, safety, and environmental implications. Additionally, if you charge extra for off-site disposal, you'll want to be well-versed in your local disposal rules and best practices.

Proper Disposal: Local Dumping Rules and Alternatives

When clients request off-site disposal, it's essential to follow local regulations to avoid fines or legal issues. Each municipality may have different rules about where pet waste can be disposed of, so it's crucial to do your research.

Options for Waste Disposal:

1. **Local Landfills or Dumps**
   - Many cities allow pet waste to be disposed of at landfills, but some may require special permits.
   - Be aware that repeated trips to the landfill increase your operational costs due to fuel and time spent driving.
2. **Transfer Stations**
   - Some areas have waste transfer stations where pet waste can be dropped off for a small fee. This can be a more convenient option than a landfill if it's closer to

your service area.

3. **Special Waste Removal Services**
   ◦ Some companies specialize in the disposal of pet waste and hazardous materials. Partnering with them can provide a reliable way to handle off-site waste removal.

4. **Customer Trash Bins (Preferred Method)**
   ◦ Encourage clients to allow you to use their household trash bins. It saves you time and ensures waste is disposed of through the city's regular waste management system.

Tip: Be transparent about extra charges for off-site disposal to avoid misunderstandings. You might charge an additional **$5-$10 per visit** for waste removal beyond the property.

Potential Environmental Uses: Is Composting Possible?

Many people wonder if pet waste can be composted for environmental benefit. Unfortunately, composting pet waste is not as straightforward as composting food scraps or plant material, due to the potential health risks associated with pet feces.

Challenges with Composting Pet Waste:

- **Harmful Bacteria and Parasites:** Dog waste can contain pathogens like E. coli, Salmonella, and roundworms, which can survive traditional composting processes.
- **Risk of Water Contamination:** If not handled properly, composting pet waste can leach harmful bacteria into nearby water sources.
- **Specialized Composting Systems Required:** Pet waste can only be safely composted using high-heat industrial

composting systems, which are not available in most residential settings.

Safe Environmental Alternatives:

- **Biodigesters:** These are specialized systems that break down organic waste, including pet waste, to produce compost or biogas. While rare, some cities or businesses may offer biodigester services.
- **Pet Waste Disposal Stations:** Some parks or communities have waste disposal stations with biodegradable bags. If available, these can be an eco-friendly way to dispose of waste during route stops.

Note: Always inform clients that while composting may seem like an eco-friendly option, it's not recommended unless managed by a professional service with the proper equipment.

Safety Considerations: Handling Aggressive Pets or Hazardous Waste

Providing pet waste removal services may occasionally present safety challenges, especially when encountering aggressive animals or hazardous situations. Implementing safety protocols ensures both your well-being and customer satisfaction.

Handling Aggressive Pets:

1. **Pre-Visit Communication:**
    - Ask clients to keep pets indoors or secured during your visit.
    - For homes with known aggressive animals, send a **text or email reminder** ahead of your arrival.

2. **Carrying Treats as a Friendly Gesture:**
    - Offering treats (with the client's approval) can help build rapport with pets.
    - Some clients appreciate this extra effort, which can make your visit smoother.
3. **Establish Boundaries:**
    - If a dog appears too aggressive, do not enter the yard. Instead, notify the client and reschedule or request the animal be secured.

Dealing with Hazardous Waste and Environmental Hazards:

- **Sharp Objects or Hazardous Trash:** Watch for broken glass, sharp objects, or hazardous waste in the areas you're cleaning.
- **Frozen Waste:** In colder climates, waste may freeze, making it harder to scoop. Offer a **spring thaw cleanup** at a higher rate to deal with accumulated winter waste.
- **Hazardous Pet Waste:** Some waste may contain parasites or blood, posing a health risk. Wear **disposable gloves** and use **sanitizing spray** on tools to reduce exposure.

Personal Protective Equipment (PPE) Recommendations:

- Gloves (disposable or reusable with proper sanitization).
- Closed-toe shoes or boots with slip-resistant soles.
- Safety glasses for protection against accidental splashes during cleaning.

Conclusion

While pet waste removal may seem straightforward, understanding the nuances of proper disposal, environmental considerations, and safety protocols is essential for running a successful business. The preferred approach is to dispose of waste in the client's trash bin, minimizing the need for off-site disposal and streamlining operations. For clients requesting off-site removal, following local regulations and charging appropriately ensures your business remains profitable and compliant.

By taking precautions to handle aggressive pets and hazardous waste, you can maintain a safe working environment. As your business grows, keeping these best practices in mind will help you provide excellent service and build trust with your clients.

Marketing and Building a Brand

Building a strong brand and executing effective marketing campaigns are essential for growing your pet waste removal business. From creating a consistent visual identity to leveraging the power of social media, community involvement, and client testimonials, a well-rounded marketing strategy will set your business apart. Additionally, small touches like matching shirts and uniforms can create a professional image that helps build trust and recognition.

Effective Branding: Consistent Colors, Logos, and Messaging

Your brand is more than just a logo—it's the story, tone, and image that customers associate with your business. In a competitive market, consistent branding helps potential clients remember you and differentiate your services from others.

Developing a Cohesive Brand Identity:

1. **Choose a Color Palette and Logo**
   - Pick two to three colors that represent your brand and use them consistently across all marketing materials. For example, black and gold convey professionalism and luxury, while green and white suggest eco-friendliness.
   - Design a simple, memorable logo that reflects your business's mission.
2. **Consistent Messaging Across Platforms**
   - Use a unified tone in your communications—whether playful, friendly, or professional.
   - Develop a tagline or slogan to reinforce your brand

message. Examples include:
"Scoop the Poop, Enjoy Your Yard."
"#1 in the #2 Business."

3. **Matching Shirts, Hoodies, and Vehicles**
    - Wearing matching uniforms or branded shirts makes your team look professional and helps establish trust.
    - Branded vehicles or magnets on your car further increase brand visibility, ensuring potential clients see your logo as you service routes.

Social Media Campaigns and Community Involvement

Social media is a powerful tool for marketing, allowing you to engage with potential clients and showcase your business in real time. Additionally, getting involved in your local community helps build trust and establishes your business as a reliable presence.

Social Media Marketing Strategies:

1. **Create Accounts on Major Platforms**
    - Focus on Facebook, Instagram, and local neighborhood apps like Nextdoor.
    - Post photos of happy pets, clean yards, and customer testimonials.
2. **Engage with Local Groups and Forums**
    - Join pet-related Facebook groups, community forums, and local small business groups. Be active without being too salesy—build relationships first.
    - Share posts about your services and special promotions when appropriate.
3. **Use Fun and Informative Content**
    - Post pet-related memes, share cleaning tips, and

showcase your team in action.

- Create videos demonstrating your work or showcasing happy clients (with permission).

Community Involvement for Increased Visibility:

- **Partner with Animal Shelters and Rescue Groups:**
    - Offer free or discounted clean-ups for foster homes or animal shelters in exchange for social media shout-outs and referrals.
- **Participate in Local Events:**
    - Sponsor dog parks, community events, or pet fairs. Set up booths and offer giveaways like branded poop bags or treats.

Leveraging Client Reviews and Testimonials for Growth

Customer reviews and word-of-mouth referrals are invaluable for growing a pet waste removal business. Encouraging satisfied clients to leave reviews helps build credibility and attract new customers.

How to Collect and Promote Reviews:

1. **Ask for Reviews After Each Service**
    - Send follow-up messages or emails thanking clients for their business and politely asking them to leave a review on Google, Yelp, or your Facebook page.
    - Offer a small incentive, such as a discount on future services, for leaving reviews.
2. **Display Testimonials on Your Website and Social Media**
    - Highlight positive reviews on your website and in your marketing materials.
    - Feature customer success stories in social media posts

to attract similar clientele.

3. **Word-of-Mouth Referrals**
   - Encourage current clients to refer friends or neighbors by offering referral discounts.
   - Example: *"Refer a neighbor and both of you get 10% off your next month!"*

Conclusion

A well-executed marketing plan and strong brand presence are essential for building a successful pet waste removal business. By developing consistent branding with matching shirts and professional logos, engaging actively on social media, and participating in local events, you'll ensure your business stands out from the competition. Leveraging customer reviews and offering referral incentives will further accelerate your growth, creating a solid foundation for long-term success.

Long-Term Growth and Scaling Strategies

Some pet waste removal businesses thrive as small, owner-operated ventures, with just one person or a tiny team handling operations. If you're content keeping things small, working flexible hours, and enjoying steady revenue, that's perfectly fine. However, if you have bigger ambitions—such as expanding your territory, adding new services, or building a team—this section will guide you through the steps needed to grow and scale your business effectively.

When and How to Expand to Nearby Cities

Expansion can be an exciting way to grow your business, but it requires careful planning. Expanding into nearby towns or cities is a natural next step once you've built a strong local customer base.

Steps to Expanding Smartly:

1. **Evaluate Your Current Market Saturation**
   - Are there still untapped opportunities in your current area? If not, it may be time to expand.
   - Consider how many homes and businesses are left to serve within your existing territory.

1. **Select Cities or Towns Strategically**
   - Start with nearby towns where travel routes are easy to manage.
   - Look for areas with high pet ownership rates and minimal competition.

2. **Test Expansion Before Committing**
   - Begin offering services once or twice a week in the

new area to gauge demand.
- Use your existing clients as referral sources to get initial customers in the new location.

3. **Create Efficient Multi-City Routes**
   - Plan routes that minimize travel time between your base city and new service areas.
   - Consider setting specific days for each town to keep routes organized.

Adding New Services or Revenue Streams

Offering additional services can help you diversify your income and strengthen customer relationships. These add-ons also provide more value to existing clients, increasing loyalty and boosting long-term revenue.

Potential Service Expansions:

1. **Deodorizing Services**
   - Offer to spray yards with pet-safe deodorizing solutions to keep outdoor spaces smelling fresh.
   - This can be marketed as a premium add-on during hot summer months when odor control is essential.

2. **Pet Sitting and Dog Walking Services**
   - Many of your current clients may need pet sitting or walking services. Offering these services allows you to increase your revenue without acquiring new customers.
   - Package deals (like weekly waste removal plus two dog walks) provide extra value.

3. **Special Event Clean-Ups**
   - Provide one-time services for outdoor parties, dog parks, or community events. These jobs are often

high-margin and can lead to additional business.

4. **Commercial Contracts**
    - Expand into contracts with apartment complexes, homeowners' associations (HOAs), and dog parks.
    - These larger contracts offer recurring revenue and reduce the need for constant client acquisition.

Hiring, Delegating, and Building a Team

Scaling your business often means hiring employees or subcontractors to handle growing demand. Expanding from a one-person operation to a team can be challenging, but it's essential if you want to grow efficiently.

Hiring Your First Employee:

1. **Know When It's Time to Hire**
    - If your workload is too much to handle alone or you want to free up time for business development, it may be time to hire.
    - Consider hiring part-time help first to ease into managing a team.
2. **Where to Find Employees**
    - Post job ads on platforms like Indeed or local Facebook job groups.
    - Consider hiring college students or part-time workers for flexibility.
3. **Training and Delegation**
    - Create clear training materials to onboard new employees quickly.
    - Use route planning software or CRMs to assign tasks and track employee progress.
4. **Managing Payroll and Legal Requirements**
    - Set up a payroll system to ensure employees are paid

> correctly and on time.
> - Make sure to comply with labor laws, including worker's compensation insurance and taxes.

Transitioning to a Leadership Role:

1. **Shift Your Focus to Management and Growth**
   - As your business grows, your role will evolve from daily operations to managing your team and expanding services.
   - Focus on developing strategies, building relationships, and finding new revenue streams.
2. **Hiring a Manager or Delegating Operations**
   - If you plan to step back from daily operations, consider hiring a manager to oversee routes and customer service.
   - Delegating responsibilities allows you to focus on long-term strategy and growth.

Conclusion

While some entrepreneurs prefer to run a lean operation and enjoy the freedom of being their own boss, others are drawn to the challenge of scaling their business. If you choose to expand, focus on strategic growth by adding nearby cities, diversifying your services, and hiring the right team. Whether you decide to keep your business small or grow it into a multi-city operation, the key to long-term success is planning, adaptability, and maintaining excellent customer service.

Real-Life Success Stories and Lessons Learned

The pet waste removal business is filled with success stories, and there are also plenty of lessons to be learned from the experiences of others. Whether you're starting independently or considering a franchise like DoodyCalls, insights from real-world entrepreneurs provide invaluable guidance. Below, we highlight some inspiring success stories, share Reddit insights, and identify common pitfalls to avoid.

Reddit Insights: What Worked and What Didn't for Other Entrepreneurs

Alex's Story (Name changed): Building a Route and Leaving a 9-to-5 Job

Alex ran a small side business scooping pet waste, intending to pick up a handful of clients for supplemental income. Within just a few months, however, he grew his customer base to 39 regular households through effective marketing and good communication.

What Worked:

- **Branding:** Alex used a professional name and logo, avoiding overly playful branding that might embarrass customers.
- **Responsive Communication:** He made responsiveness a priority, answering inquiries quickly and building trust with clients.
- **Word-of-Mouth and Flyers:** Posting flyers at vet clinics and animal shelters led to a steady stream of new clients.

Lesson Learned: Alex's experience shows the power of branding and being responsive. His decision to keep his pricing low initially helped attract clients, but it also taught him that raising prices gradually was necessary to maintain profit margins.

Lisa's Story (Name changed): Adding Services for Long-Term Growth

Lisa initially started with pet waste removal but found it easy to add other services like pet sitting and dog walking. Over the first year, she grew her business to $6,000 per month, mostly by upselling current clients to additional services.

What Worked:

- **Service Expansion:** Offering multiple pet-related services provided more income streams and client loyalty.
- **Email Newsletters:** Lisa used monthly newsletters to update clients about her services, promote events, and offer discounts.

Lesson Learned: Lisa found that keeping operations organized was key. Her experience illustrates that diversifying services can increase revenue while deepening relationships with clients.

Mark's Story (Name changed): Pricing Challenges and Scaling Issues

Mark priced his services low to gain customers quickly, but he soon found that his margins were too thin to cover travel costs and vehicle maintenance. Despite acquiring many clients, the profit didn't justify the workload. He eventually adjusted his pricing structure based on yard size, dog count, and travel distance, which allowed him to continue scaling.

What Worked:

- **Client Acquisition:** Offering low introductory rates helped Mark gain clients quickly.
- **Adaptability:** Mark realized early on that his pricing model needed to change, and he pivoted before losing too much money.

Pitfall to Avoid: Underpricing services can lead to burnout and financial losses. It's essential to strike a balance between competitive pricing and maintaining profitability.

DoodyCalls Case Study: A Franchise Success Story

DoodyCalls began in 2000 when founder Jacob D'Aniello saw an opportunity in pet waste management. Today, the franchise has grown to over 40 territories nationwide, serving residential and commercial clients with a focus on customer satisfaction and professionalism.

Why DoodyCalls Succeeded:

- **Recurring Revenue:** Their subscription-based model ensured consistent, predictable income.
- **Technology Integration:** With proprietary software like PoopNET, they streamlined scheduling, customer management, and invoicing.
- **Community Involvement:** DoodyCalls fostered positive relationships with local organizations, including animal shelters and HOAs.

Lessons from DoodyCalls:

The success of DoodyCalls highlights the importance of standardized operations, effective branding, and leveraging technology to improve efficiency. Aspiring entrepreneurs can learn from their example by investing in scheduling tools and building relationships with local communities.

Pitfalls to Avoid: Learning from Failures in the Industry

Common Mistakes Entrepreneurs Make

1. **Underpricing Services:**
   Entrepreneurs often price their services too low to attract clients but find themselves struggling to cover costs. Learn from Mark's (Name changed) mistake—price your services carefully based on costs and competition.

2. **Poor Route Planning:**
   Failing to plan routes efficiently leads to increased travel time and fuel costs. Tools like Google Maps or specialized CRM systems can prevent this issue.

3. **Ignoring Legal Requirements:**
   Skipping insurance or failing to register the business properly can lead to fines and legal trouble down the line. Always check local regulations and ensure you have adequate insurance coverage.

4. **Overexpansion Without Structure:**
   Expanding too quickly, especially to distant cities, can cause logistical nightmares. Make sure your processes are streamlined before taking on new territories.

5. **Inconsistent Branding and Communication:**
   Consistency in branding and responsiveness builds trust. Lisa (Name changed) and Alex (Name changed) succeeded by ensuring they stayed professional and responsive to their clients' needs.

Conclusion: Learning from Others' Experiences

The stories of Alex, Lisa, Mark, and the success of DoodyCalls provide valuable insights into building and scaling a pet waste removal business. Whether you plan to keep things small or grow into a regional service, the key to long-term success lies in smart pricing, strong client relationships, efficient operations, and adaptability. With these lessons in mind, you'll be better prepared to avoid common pitfalls and capitalize on opportunities in the pet waste management industry.

Financial Management and Tracking Profits

Managing the financial side of your pet waste removal business is crucial to long-term success. It's not just about bringing in money; you also need to manage expenses, track profits, and ensure smooth cash flow. In this chapter, we'll cover how to handle cash flow, the benefits of using accounting software, and methods for tracking profits across routes and service areas.

Managing Cash Flow and Recurring Payments

Cash flow refers to the money coming in and going out of your business. Even if your pet waste removal business brings in steady revenue, managing cash flow ensures you always have enough to cover expenses like fuel, vehicle maintenance, insurance, and payroll (if applicable). Here are some tips to help:

- **Automate Recurring Payments:**
  With a subscription-based model, most of your clients will pay you on a weekly or monthly basis. Automating payments through platforms like PayPal, Stripe, or Square ensures timely payments and minimizes administrative work.
- **Offer Multiple Payment Options:**
  Provide clients with options such as credit cards, ACH transfers, or mobile payments (e.g., Venmo, Apple Pay). This flexibility makes it easier for them to pay on time.
- **Create a Buffer Fund:**
  Since expenses like fuel and vehicle repairs can fluctuate, it's a good idea to maintain a cash reserve. Aim to save enough to

cover at least two to three months of operating expenses.

- **Track Late Payments:**
  While most clients will pay on time, some may forget or encounter issues. Establish a system to monitor overdue payments and send polite reminders. Offering a small discount for timely payments or charging a late fee can help motivate timely payments.

Using Accounting Software for Small Businesses

As your business grows, manually tracking expenses and profits becomes unsustainable. Using accounting software makes it easier to manage finances, file taxes, and track performance metrics. Below are some options to consider:

Popular Accounting Software

- **QuickBooks Online:** A comprehensive tool for invoicing, tracking income and expenses, and generating financial reports. It integrates with payment platforms to streamline transactions.
- **Wave:** A free accounting tool suitable for small businesses, especially those just starting out. Wave handles basic bookkeeping, invoicing, and payment tracking.
- **FreshBooks:** This software offers easy-to-use invoicing and time-tracking features, ideal if you expand your services to include pet sitting or dog walking.
- **Zoho Books:** Zoho provides affordable plans for small businesses with features like expense tracking, tax reports, and project management.

Benefits of Using Software

- **Accurate Financial Reporting:** Quickly generate profit and loss statements, cash flow reports, and balance sheets.
- **Simplified Tax Filing:** Track deductible expenses (e.g., fuel, equipment) to make tax season easier.
- **Expense Categorization:** Break down expenses into categories such as supplies, vehicle costs, and marketing for better analysis.
- **Automated Invoicing:** Set up recurring invoices for subscription clients and receive alerts for overdue payments.

Tracking Profits per Route and Service Area

Knowing which routes and services are most profitable is essential for scaling your business efficiently. Here are some strategies to help you track profits by route and service area:

- **Calculate Profit per Route:**
  Track the revenue and expenses for each route, including fuel and vehicle wear-and-tear costs. You may find that some routes are more profitable than others due to factors like proximity and the number of clients.

Example Calculation:

- Total revenue for Route A: $500/week
- Fuel costs: $50
- Wear and tear: $20
- Profit: $430/week

- **Monitor Profitability by Service Type:**
  Track how much revenue each service generates (e.g., weekly subscriptions, one-time cleanups, or deodorizing). Use this information to focus on high-margin services and decide whether to adjust pricing for lower-margin offerings.

- **Use a CRM or Spreadsheet for Tracking:**
  Tools like Google Sheets or specialized CRMs like PoopNET make it easy to log revenue and expenses per client, route, and service area. This helps you understand which areas are growing and which may need improvement.
- **Seasonal Adjustments:**
  In colder climates, business may slow during the winter. Track revenue trends over time to identify seasonal patterns. This information can guide your marketing efforts and help you plan for slower months by offering promotions or shifting your focus to other services.

- **Measure Key Metrics:**
  Keep an eye on performance indicators like:
    - **Average revenue per client**
    - **Number of new clients per month**
    - **Customer retention rate**
    - **Cost per mile (fuel, wear, and tear)**

Monitoring these metrics will give you a clear picture of your business's financial health and highlight areas for improvement.

Conclusion: Financial Management for Long-Term Success

Managing your finances effectively ensures that your pet waste removal business remains profitable and sustainable. Automating payments, using accounting software, and carefully tracking profits per route and service area will help you stay organized and identify growth opportunities. By staying on top of cash flow and expenses, you'll be better prepared to handle challenges and scale your business when the time is right.

Legal Considerations and Permits

In many areas, running a pet waste removal business can be as straightforward as picking up waste and disposing of it in the client's trash. However, it's essential to familiarize yourself with local regulations and understand the legalities involved, particularly if you plan to work with commercial clients or scale your business. While not every location will require permits or specific compliance measures, knowing the legal landscape ensures you avoid potential trouble down the road.

Local Regulations for Waste Disposal

Disposing of pet waste improperly can lead to fines or environmental violations, especially if you transport waste off-site. Here are a few points to consider:

- **Disposing in Clients' Trash:**
  This is the easiest and most cost-effective method if allowed in your area. Always check with local ordinances to ensure there are no restrictions against disposing of pet waste in residential bins.
- **Dumping Rules at Landfills:**
  If you collect and transport waste yourself, confirm with your local waste management authority whether the landfill or transfer station accepts pet waste. Some areas may classify it as hazardous or require special handling.
- **Special Waste Handling Requirements:**
  Some jurisdictions require the use of biodegradable bags or may restrict disposal methods for large amounts of waste. Make sure you're aware of any rules regarding bag types or waste

separation, particularly if you serve commercial properties.

- **Environmental Protection Measures:**
Avoid improper disposal in storm drains, vacant lots, or public spaces, which can lead to legal penalties and damage to your business reputation.

Special Considerations for Commercial Contracts

When working with commercial clients like apartment complexes, HOAs, or parks, additional legal considerations may apply:

- **Insurance Requirements:**
Many commercial clients will require proof of insurance, including general liability coverage and possibly vehicle insurance, to ensure you're covered in case of accidents or damages on their property.
- **Written Contracts:**
Having a formal contract in place for commercial clients helps protect both parties and clarifies the scope of services, payment terms, and liability. These contracts may also include clauses related to access, hours of operation, or pet safety.
- **Compliance with Property Rules:**
Some properties, especially HOAs, may have specific rules about waste disposal or access to shared areas. Make sure you understand these policies before agreeing to provide services.
- **Health and Safety Regulations:**
Commercial clients may be subject to stricter regulations for cleanliness and waste management. Ensure your services align with their legal obligations to avoid disputes.

Staying Compliant and Avoiding Legal Trouble

Being proactive about compliance can prevent costly mistakes and protect your reputation. Here are some best practices:

- **Business License:**
  Even if you're a sole proprietor, many municipalities require a basic business license. Check with your city or county clerk's office for requirements.
- **Liability Insurance:**
  General liability insurance is a must for pet waste removal businesses. It protects you from claims related to property damage, injuries, or accidents during service.
- **Waivers and Agreements:**
  If you encounter aggressive pets or hazardous waste situations, having liability waivers for clients can protect you from potential legal claims.
- **Record Keeping:**
  Keep records of your service agreements, disposal methods, and any client communication. Good documentation will protect you in case of disputes or audits.
- **Ongoing Compliance Checks:**
  Regulations can change, so it's wise to periodically review local ordinances and landfill rules to ensure you're staying compliant. Join industry groups or online communities to stay informed about any legal updates.

Conclusion: Stay Informed, Stay Protected

Although pet waste removal may not involve heavy regulatory burdens, being aware of potential legal requirements ensures that your business operates smoothly and avoids unnecessary risks. Whether it's confirming that you can dispose of waste in clients' trash or securing liability insurance for commercial contracts, staying proactive will help you protect your business and build trust with your clients. While you may not need every legal measure mentioned here, having this knowledge in your back pocket ensures you're prepared as your business grows.

Conclusion

Congratulations! You've reached the final chapter of this guide, and by now, you have a complete understanding of what it takes to launch, manage, and grow a successful pet waste removal business. This venture, while unconventional, offers incredible opportunities for flexible work, recurring revenue, and personal satisfaction. Whether you're looking to start small with a solo operation or scale up with multiple employees and service areas, you now have the tools and knowledge to turn your business dreams into reality.

A Recap of the Journey

Let's take a moment to reflect on what we've covered in this book and the key steps that will guide you on your entrepreneurial journey.

The Opportunity in Pet Waste Removal

We began by discussing the booming demand for pet waste removal services. With more households adopting pets than ever before, this industry presents a prime opportunity for those willing to roll up their sleeves and build a service-based business. The recurring nature of the work ensures steady income, and the flexibility of managing your own schedule makes it an ideal business model for those seeking work-life balance.

Business Structure and Legal Setup

Choosing the right business structure was the next critical step. Whether you opt for a sole proprietorship, LLC, or S-Corp, the structure impacts your liability, taxes, and long-term growth potential. We also explored the importance of obtaining the necessary business licenses and insurance to protect yourself and your clients.

Planning, Tools, and Startup Costs

We discussed the value of creating a business plan—even if you're not seeking external funding. Setting goals, defining services, and forecasting revenue give you a roadmap to follow. We then moved into the practical side: the minimal equipment needed to get started, such as scoopers, bags, and transportation. You learned how low startup costs can make this business accessible to nearly anyone, and we covered optional items like deodorizing spray and customer gifts to set yourself apart.

Finding and Retaining Clients

Securing your first clients is often the biggest challenge for new business owners. We explored strategies for marketing, including social media campaigns, partnerships with animal shelters, and good old-fashioned flyers. Communication and responsiveness are key to building lasting client relationships, and we showed how being reliable can lead to word-of-mouth referrals and customer loyalty.

Pricing Services and Managing Routes

Setting the right prices is an art. We discussed how to base pricing on factors like the number of dogs, frequency of visits, and regional market conditions. Reddit insights gave us real-world pricing examples, showing how businesses across the country structure their rates. We also emphasized the importance of efficient route planning, using tools like Google Maps or CRM systems to minimize travel time and maximize profits.

Operations, Scaling, and Managing Growth

For those who want to keep the business small and manageable, running solo with a handful of clients may be the perfect fit. But if you're ready to grow, we outlined strategies for hiring employees, subcontracting labor, and expanding into new territories. You now know how to upsell related services—like dog walking, pet sitting, and deodorizing treatments—to boost revenue streams.

Handling Pet Waste Safely and Legally

Proper disposal of pet waste is critical, both for maintaining a positive reputation and staying compliant with local regulations. While many businesses can simply dispose of waste in the client's trash bin, we also explored more complex options like transporting waste to dumps or composting. Safety considerations, such as dealing with aggressive pets and hazardous waste, were also covered.

Branding, Marketing, and Reviews

A consistent brand identity helps set your business apart. We discussed the importance of using matching shirts, logos, and social media campaigns to project professionalism. Community involvement, positive client reviews, and testimonials serve as powerful marketing tools that help you stand out from competitors.

Managing Finances and Legal Compliance

We addressed the importance of managing cash flow, using accounting software, and tracking profits by route or service area. Staying on top of legal requirements—like obtaining the right permits and insurance—is essential for long-term success. Although the regulations are often straightforward, knowing what's required ensures you avoid costly mistakes.

Learning from Success Stories and Mistakes

Throughout this book, we shared real-life insights from Reddit users and case studies, highlighting what works and what doesn't in the pet waste removal business. From building efficient routes to overcoming common challenges, these stories offer valuable lessons that can guide your decisions as you grow your business.

Taking the First Step Toward Success

Starting a business is always a leap of faith, but you now have a clear path to follow. Whether your goal is to earn some extra income on the side or build a full-fledged business with multiple routes and employees, this book provides the blueprint you need to succeed. The beauty of the pet waste removal business is its simplicity—low startup costs, minimal equipment, and recurring revenue make it one of the most accessible service businesses out there.

Adapting and Growing Along the Way

While this guide offers a comprehensive framework, every business is unique. You'll encounter challenges and opportunities that require you to adapt your strategies. The key is to stay flexible, listen to client feedback, and refine your processes as you grow. Whether you decide to keep things small or pursue expansion, the tools and insights in this book will serve as your foundation.

The Road Ahead: A Business That Works for You

At the heart of this business is freedom—the freedom to choose your schedule, grow at your own pace, and create a service that aligns with your lifestyle. Whether you're working alone or managing a team, you have the power to design the business that works best for you. With a focus on excellent customer service, efficient operations, and smart financial management, your pet waste removal business can become not just a job, but a fulfilling career.

Closing Thoughts: Ready to Scoop Up Success?

The journey to success starts with a single step, and now you're armed with the knowledge to take that step confidently. This business may be about scooping waste, but it's also about creating value—both for your clients and for yourself. With persistence, adaptability, and the strategies outlined in this book, you're well-positioned to build a thriving pet waste removal business.

So what are you waiting for? Whether it's launching your first marketing campaign, planning your route, or signing your first client, the time to start is now. Scoop by scoop, client by client, your business will grow. And with it, so will your opportunities for financial freedom, personal satisfaction, and long-term success.

Good luck on your journey—and welcome to the world of pet waste removal entrepreneurship!